10 Hyde Park Gate South
Kensington
March 5th 1863.

My Dear Mr Crawfurd

Mr Corbould has spoken to me about the Prince of Wales' feathers in reply to which I am to tell you what the Prince told me respecting the drawing: "I domulate that manque compositen the taste of the Scraps & what it is my be part of a manuscript admired as the representation of the feathers thing."

H R H will have enough of that which I desire — for it seems so very very ever glaring the three feathers which I may hung up all over London & Windsor. Now the Prince as much admires the true feathers as worn by the King of Bohemen who was slain at Cressy (Crecy it was)

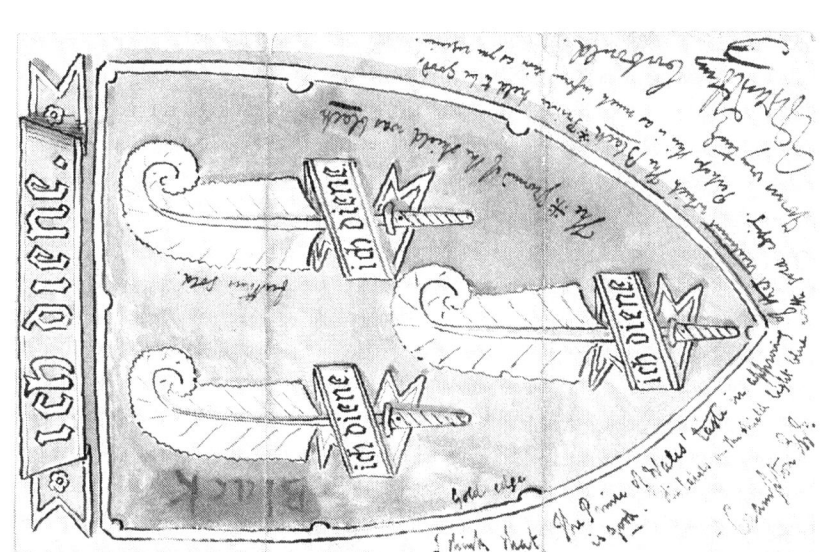

I have a desire to see it... is no other ground — the easiest to bring to the test for a letter than the matter, the King of Bohemia... (all the pursuivants of Bohemia) are there... & the Bottle pool... has nothing at all... Mr. ... the ... with the ... it is as good to get...

I have said that the King of Bohemia was there, but as I have said the pursuivants interested... Prince of Wales & the Queen? Isn't there... an interest to go with the Princess in... the King did not see the matter, but his Knights... — 1st Scene — "I grow" — the Prince of Wales say, joining... together the King in... each kingdom... bore the motto "I grow"... in P.W. who "who said the P. of Wales... an arm? He acknowledged it? And did the Prince... down... answer "The King of Wales..." however that is not the... I wish to suppose one... the further Knights were priceless. Nelson... only I give it best as you may... the arms of Prince of Wales... I behold the 3rd...

and from it must be a "D.", and from your humble to my wife.

G.H.C.

I have seen King George of Hanover dining with one in others... I have said that the King of Bohemia... Bottle as I suppose them on half park side.

NEW ITEM

NEW ITEM

NEW ITEM

31 Rutland Gate Hyde Park

Sir

The subject is landscape way — I could wish to have drawn it on the block myself — but yet scarcely see how I am to scrape together the time — seeing that I have already in hand much more than I can manage in the time. If however (if you supply the word) you could send me a block of the largest size the space will allow — I will do my best. Meantime

I am
Sir Yours very truly
Edward Henry Corbould

Joseph L. Williams Esq.

21 Rutland Gate
Hyde Park

Mr Bishop

Can you come &
me for about 3 hours on
Wednesday or tomorrow? Or
perhaps you will let me know
whether you can come when it
suits you. Believe me,
ever yours, Rudolph Lehmann.

Tuesday.

NEW ITEM

This is in Mr. Kent's autograph —

Edward Henry Corbould's
answer to me
at
Knebworth
about Drawings of [illegible]

Eldon Lodge. 29 Victoria Road. Kensington

To Charles Kent Esq. &c &. . May 4th 1882.

Dear Sir   I am in receipt of your letter of
yesterday's date — & will to the best of my ability — say
how it came to pass that I illustrated Lord Lytton's
"Lost tales of Miletus". For some years I used to paint
for two houses (almost exclusively). One was at Osborne
— and owned by Her Majesty: whilst the other was at Belper
& owned by my friend George H. Strutt. Time came, when
there remained no wall spaces whereupon to hang a
work of Art — (though occasionally I do even now paint
a picture — wh. necessitates the removal of some other
in order to make room for it.) How many pictures there
may be of mine in the Isle of Wight, at Osborne, I do not
know — but it amounts to a goodly few: whilst at Belper
in Derbysh. — pictures cover the walls of the staircase, wh.
is well & splendidly lighted. Two of my pictures have to be
placed on easels in two of the rooms — but where the
picture of Mazeppa (at present in the Institute of Painters,
in Water Colours) is to be hung — I have not the faintest idea.
The Queen has before now said to me "If I see a picture of
yours — wh. I would wish to possess — it generally turns out
to have been commissioned by Mrs Strutt! Mrs Strutt
therefore — stands in my way!"   Latterly — for

want of Wall space — the Strutt's have had some favourite books illustrated — not in colours — but in ordinary Office ink. In this way I did a set to be bound up with a large copy (broad margin) of Tennyson's "Idyls of the Kynge" &c and The lost tales of Miletus. Her Majesty wished to see these illustrations to Tennyson, & accordingly I wrote to borrow them. Mr & Mrs Strutt were about to start for Switzerland — so they at once brought them to London — and as I had to go to Osborne, I took them there. The Queen was pleased to be pleased with them, & asked me whether I thought Mrs Strutt wd object to Her having them photographed — in order to bind up with her copy? and I said that Mrs Strutt was not in England, but that I was quite certain that she wd be content with Her Majesty doing as she pleased in the matter. The Queen had suggested — the taking a single set — for one copy of the Poets work — but acting upon the notion that Mrs Strutt would raise no objection of any kind — large sets and smaller sets were taken — and thus every one of the Royal family had them, — a set were sent to me, & some sets large & small were forwarded to Belper. The Queen afterwards had a dozen pictures taken down from the Walls at Osborne — & photographed by Jabez Hughes of Ryde. — & sent them to Mrs Strutt, who again in

her term had the illustrations to Lord Lytton's "Lost
tales of Miletus" 12 in number — photographed and
sent them to Her Majesty. I conclude therefore
that the illustrations you allude to — are photographs
from my ink illustrations to Lord Lytton's work —
but whether sent to his lordship by the Queen or
by Mrs Stuart — I am quite unable to say.
Doubtless there are gross errors in some of them,
for candidly speaking — I had never read the
Lost tales — when I was called upon to illustrate them.
No artist — ought to attempt to render either
the writings of the late Lord Lytton, or Alfd Tennyson
without seriously studying the subject to get at the
true feeling of the Poet. You express a wish to know
"the circumstances under which they were originally
produced, whether they were pencilled with a view
to publication, whether in fact the idea of the
series originated with Author, Artist, or Publisher."
From what I have stated — you will gather how
it all came to pass —— though possibly I have
so jumbled the matter — that after all, you may be
almost as much in doubt — as though I had never written.
Yours very sincerely Edward Henry Corbould

P.S   Should this explanation prove insufficient — I beg you will not hesitate to say so — and I will then endeavour to obtain a more substantial version from head quarters.   I have but the one set of photos wh. were sent to me — but had I a duplicate set — I should at once have sent them to you for yourself. (as you appear to have taken so much interest in the subject) — & then you could have satisfied yourself as to whether they are identical with those found in the portfolio of drawings at Knebworth Park. At any time I shall be most happy to furnish particulars & talk over matters of any kind within my ken. & am mostly to be found at all hours here in my den. Campden Grove is not far from this part of Kensington.

NEW ITEM

2 Edwardes Lodge, Victoria Road
Kensington. April 13th 1878.

To Mr Joseph Mallett.

Dr Sir - I have this afternoon
received your Nos (the Octavo Contralti)
first note from Australia - in which
he says - among other things "I wish Mr
Mallett where Penalty Established
is somewhere in Western Aust. &c.
not to trash up the type for Catalogue
by John Martin & all Supplement -
Pictures - N also that Mr Cooper
who printed the key plate for same)
would not destroy the plate - as I
may require some more printed here
from - in fact may have to write before this
note reaches you." -- I've been

The Case – perhaps you would beg
look to the matter – so that even
should such a trifling order suddenly
come – that 500 – or 5,000

Copies are required for the French
off – and packed in a box, with
Mr. Livesey ————— the order may
not come to anything, as I feel
you totally unprepared to execute
it forthwith. The order has not yet been
– but enough from anything for days may
come to me enough – when you shall
hear from me immediately –

Yours very truly
Edward King Ormonde..

NEW ITEM

W. W. De La Rue

110 Bunhill Row

June 17th   1879.

NEW ITEM

Eldon Lodge. Victoria R.d Kensington.

Dear Sir   August 29th 1874.

                    Respecting the designs for the
Middlemarch B.k Note – it would seem that
since no one is exactly able to say precisely
what it ought to consist of – the way would
be to come at it from the opposite direction
– by finding out what to avoid making it.
I have thought a great deal on the subject
as to what would be best, but have arrived
at nothing remarkably good or definite.
I will, in the course of two or three days send
you a sketch or two, w.h may possibly tend to
suggest something of a wholly different character,
but whatever suggestions may come from your
house shall be treated with the utmost care
here. There is not so great a difficulty in
managing the small circles as the larger one

Of a subject that could not appear well
for a Bank note - I have enclosed you
One Cast from one of the Nothern Museums
into the waste paper basket.

For the next week, I shall be what
at work as possible - it being in the End
is a gale of wind - is not I confess
something I have in hand - how to my
leaving town.   I filled away I will
It is very well not to neglect your business
although I go for relaxation & pleasure
I start next Saturday afternoon. It So
out & Margate - Sorry at first when I
shall stay for some weeks & then go to the coast.
My brother Dr Cox will reside at Ryde - he will
attend to me at Scarning Lodge (his house) will
be handed from me - I go with my friend &
are now to remain & are accompanied with the Climate
we shall see it - time will to... then Ismailia place.

These are if in time & while last of subject
which if written down within circles - would soon
begin to take such shape in your mind as to enable
you to advance step by step - until you
were able to say - we want such & such

subjects sketched out - in order that
we may
arrive at some definite conclusion.
And upon that - it is most likely that
I should be able without much difficulty to meet
your wishes. This I think will be altogether the best
& by the shortest way, that method which I
at first suggested - by making drawings of all
sorts of things - until it last their importance,
that if I found somewhat nearer the mark -
it be a long round about way - tiresome to me
& without profit to you. One simple example

There will be no need for you to send any immediate reply to this. The only matter for consideration at present — is, whether heads of those who caused so much trouble to the great Caesar — viz CASSIVELAVNUS & BOADICEA would be suitable for circles and if so — what subject wd be for the upright. It is no very easy matter to settle upon the subject nor is it too easy to make the design, when the subject is determined on. — for instance — what is more easy than to say "We will have Boadicea the Queen of the Iceni in a chariot with her two daughters, surrounded by her half wild British Troops; and we wish you to show upon a rising ground, in a chariot — Caesar surrounded by his Cohorts &c (?) However you may at all times rely on my endeavour to do the best in your service. Sometimes I can't do a stroke for anyone but myself, but that is not just at present! At present I am yours obediently

Edward W. B. Corbould &c

H. W. De La Rue Esq.

NEW ITEM

Ellora Lodge, Victoria Road,
Leamington. Feby. 8th 1872.

Sir,

Anxious to get places in Life Studies on the day of the Ceremony — for myself, wife & nieces I refer the trouble of 20 years service in the Royal Household — H.R.H. The Prince of Wales having one of my pupils) work & Osborne — as all that time — no information had been publicly made known through the Times — for 7 or 8 / but was not I believe sent at the present moment — and not of the enclosure — and the enclosure is...

the subject.

May I ask your kindness to
.... you can of course send my reply ..?
I am aware that there will be ....
persons brought about this time — as to such
... persons anxious? I have the honor to be

Your very obdt servant
Edward Henry Corbould.

To The Lord Chamberlain

NEW ITEM

Eldon Lodge. Victoria Road. Kensington

to The Chevalier de Chatelain   12th March 1870.

My dear Sir,

Having "nothing to wear" ex-
-cept it be a suit of Henry 7th armour.
I wish to ask as a favor. that on Tuesday
next I may ~~be able to~~ have the use if were so
small a room (bath room. any thing) in which
I may be able to retire in order to change
the very heavy steel from a suit of evening
dress. I shall bring with me a small port-
-manteau containing the change. but shall be
at your house on that night. As a true knight ought.

Yours very truly
Edwin Henry Corbould

NEW ITEM

Elstree Lodge. Victoria Road. Kensington. Home of Guests Parker

First May - 1872.

Dear Ward

The result of your investigation (the work of art
(supposed to have been painted by your father) I have communicated to my
brother-in-law at Rome — and have this morning received from him a letter in
reply — where he says that your verdict being merely & your judgment, what it
has been — the very next thing for him to suppose is — that he will have to pay the best
£5! By the way I did ask myself from the best £5 you sent by L.P.D.C. & I
thought my wife did — but she told me she did not — that when it arrives, it was
a statute of any father's structure — All the words were - that you write £5, because

NEW ITEM

Eldon Lodge. Victoria Road. Kensington. ye eve of Guido Fawkes hys daye 1872.

Dear Ward   I regret that I have not a heap of Royal Autographs to forward to you! You see the matter stands just thus — where I have letters — written from the Queen - The Prince of Wales - The Princess Royal F.W. of Prussia, Princess Alice Hesse Darmstadt or Princess Louisa — those letters are important to me or my family only, & if I cut out the name — those writings are of no value to anyone from the fact of the name of the writer being wanting. You will see the force of the argument & understand how it is that I am unable to supply the demand   Yours very truly

George Raphael Ward Esq.   Edward Henry Corbould.

NEW ITEM

The Prince [illegible]
Kensington Palace
June 2 1864

My Provost

For a long Time. I have known Pickersgill[?] ...
before [illegible] Providence furnished the supply
of [illegible] it myself. As I may find
I could [illegible] my way here by [illegible] on the
[illegible] stages — if nothing of an over[illegible]
nature came between to prevent —
[illegible] I meet you. I have [illegible]
[illegible] of your concerns. The [illegible] who [illegible] met
as in last Saturday in [illegible]
[illegible]
[illegible] him [illegible]
[illegible]

NEW ITEM

The Prince of Wales Toram

Kensington Palace

Jan 28 1865

Myster Mr Evans

I inclose a cheque for the two Drawings

I am sorry I send ... and R I have tried

heard for the Drawings 1 & 3. 11.6 you

could not have been more kind it is only

it. Why so much have I tried it off. the

any minute the drawings I sent into you

Believe me ... I accept the Thanks of

Yours very truly

Edward Henry Corbould

Edmund Evans Esqr

NEW ITEM

.

NEW ITEM

10 Major Park Ct S.W.

18th Oct 1862.

My dear Sir

I regret I am unable to
tell you in the matter upon which you had
expressed. I very much regret it. I shall
although I am personally favourable, there
are then who can render you my thanks
help in the hope of procuring information &c.
for very obliging it to the best I can hold
and I shall very glad at any time of
order — if to the [illegible] had.

Why not them go to my friend Warren the
Police General of the Kings Hill Constabulary
for place — Metropolitan Houses — Chelsea

N

Kings Road

Church St

(this is the Kings Road Entrance)

NEW ITEM

NEW ITEM

Institute of Painters
in Water Colours
Founded 1831
Gallery 53 Pall Mall.

Feb. 4th 1867

Dear William,

Although I had received a telegram from
brother's (Richard's) wife to say that he was
fast approaching his end, & had expressed a
desire to see me — I postponed going down
to Sydenham till tomorrow — owing to a desire to
act towards you here this evening. Your works
sent were received with great pleasure by the
members, and were considered as a tremendous
stride in the right direction — Nevertheless
the votes just fell short of the proper number.
I cannot tell you how greatly I felt disappointed
at such an unlooked for result!

You could not any how feel more so than I did. However it may be a sort of consolation to hear that the same fate attended the election of the son (aged 30) of one of our oldest & most highly esteemed members. as well as many others who were proposed &c. Your drawings certainly took a far higher standing than any others which were brought before the members. I felt so confident of your election, that my disappointment was proportionately great. I dont know whether I ought to lure you forward & try again — I am thoroughly disgusted and will therefore say no more, but leave the matter in your hands. Yours very truly

Edward Henry Corbould.

William C. Williams Esq.

Joseph L. Williams Esq.
22 Victoria Road,
Edward Hay (cortinued)

NEW ITEM

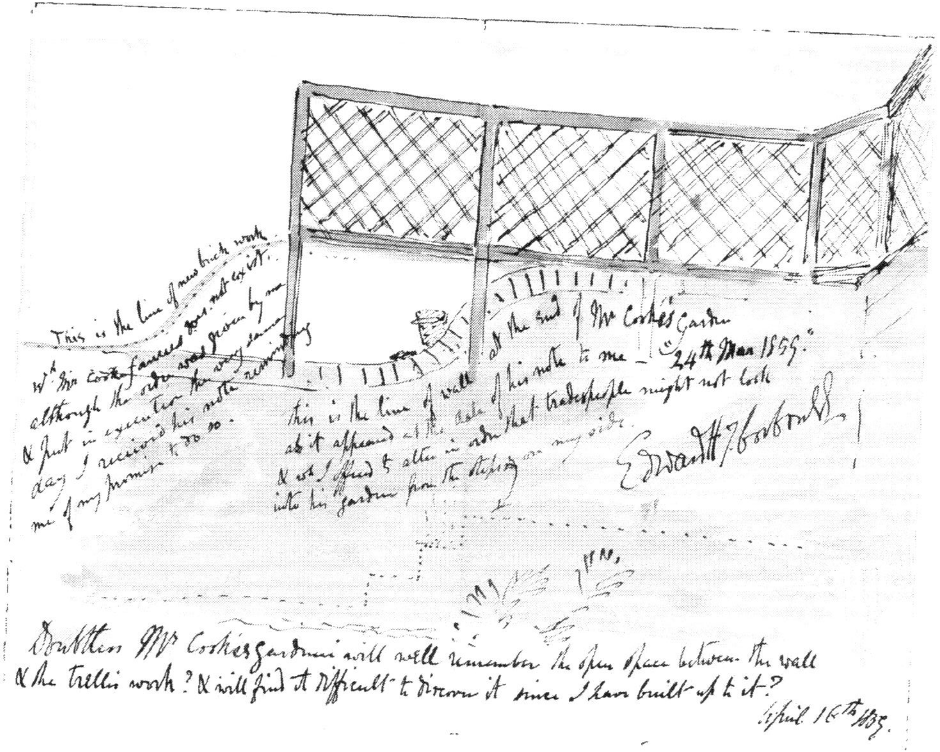
This is the line of new brick work
wh Mr Cooke fancies does not exist.
although the order was given by me
& just in execution the very same
day I received his note reminding
me of my promise to do so.
this is the line of wall at the end of Mr Cooke's Garden
as it appeared at the date of his note to me – "24th Mar 1855."
& wh I offered to alter in order that tradespeople might not look
into his garden from the steps on my side.
Edward H Cockrell
Doubtless Mr Cooke's gardener will well remember the open space between the wall
& the trellis work? & will find it difficult to discover it since I have built up to it?
April 16th 1855.

NEW ITEM

Stanhope Gate, Hyde Park
30th Dec 1873

My Dear Sir,

I delivered the Book
Commander in Chief to the
hands of H.R.H The Prince of Wales
at the Levee yesterday. He passed
it Season's Compliments. The American Sales
have not as yet, I imagine, appeared
before the Public yet etc.

Yours very truly
Edward Dalziel Brothers

Edward Dalziel Bro.

NEW ITEM

6th Jany 1858 — Rutland Gate Hyde Park

I have received the two guineas & ha. of for
the design of .... the "Harold"
Edward .... for Books

The above sketch is a genuine one. The regular
receipt stamp is but a copy from a drawing of mine

Geo. .... Edmund Evans ...

NEW ITEM

10 Of Hyde Park Gate South,
The Queen's Gate.
Kensington.
Friday Even'g 7th May.

My dear Sir

The Princess Alice having
made a sketch from your representation
of "King Lear" – and being desirous of
making a drawing for the Queen
(to be kept a secret till after it is pre-
sented on 24th inst.) requested me
this afternoon to witness the scene
that I might more fully understand
her feeling of the subject, and thus be
enabled to render her such trifling aid as
occasion might suggest. For this purpose
I have come in the hope that there may
be a corner of your box into which you
would allow me to creep. & from which

P.S. If it is in the smallest degree inconvenient this evening, or in the places if filled up, I'll by no means disturb the notice "No" & I shall be content.

If I fail to get room this place (certainly the house is very often filled up mostly), I shall at all events be able to witness the Scenes "Lerant & Keans", but the Theatre was quite full before I got there.

Charles Kean

point I should see it pretty much
the same as the Queen would
view it from Her box above.

I have considered that by writing
this line I should be less an interrup-
tion to you — than by forcing myself
into your august presence to ask
the question.

Respecting your kindness in sending a
box ticket some weeks back — I acted
under the impression that Mrs Corbould was
going to write & thank you — until time
had passed on — when I felt it was too late
& was consequently ashamed of writing.

Yours very truly
Edward Henry Corbould

Colonel ?

NEW ITEM

It was on the thirteenth day of April 1858, that Mr. Edmund Evans landed on the two pinnies & a half for a drive for "Russell" —

[signature]

NEW ITEM

.

J Fyncherie. Douglas Aug't 31. 55.

"M' Lewis dear"

I should have been overjoyed at
the prospect of going round the Island with you
this morning. but the fact is. that the work
I have to do for the Illustrated News (who are
like the lords of the Medes & Persians and wont
wait, _I did so my self before._ I have promised to execute their wishes
and am consequently forced to stay. else they
will be thrown out sadly in their calculations.

Scarcely can one expect to have such another day
is likely. the calm. the Packet going round. and a fellow
at hand ready & willing "to do just so." Accept the thanks
& wishes that a luckless day may attend all my years) of

Yours very truly _____

NEW ITEM

27th Nov 59

Dear Sir

It is not very convenient
to send von so small a sum as
15/- today - owing to my having
to pay a larger sum this evening
& will carry away very [?]
am possessed of at present - but
[?] and someone for the annexed
half sheet in the course of a few
days.

Yours [?]
[signature]

179 Regent Street

Monday 185

My dear Sir

The Chair will
resume from the
account of the measure
as chairman will be
thirteen enough to
one of two next
month

Yours very truly

NEW ITEM

21 Rutland Gate, Hyde Park

29 Nov 1852.

My Dear Sir,

I received this morning your...

If you wish it — I would send...

The pleasure [...] purchased by Boys together with one [...] time for my Sunday pictures called the Shield of the Field, which was [...] paid for time for my Sunday pictures [...] Dorothy — in fact I may say the [...] there was a companion picture [...] very down side is a [...] — I was repaid at the same time [...] it was called "Mary Ann" this was [...]

NEW ITEM

Dear Sir,

I beg to acknowledge the receipt of
five guineas from the hearing of the songs for the
Illustrated London News. 19th Dec 1852.

£5.5.

Edward W.S. Gosling.

Richmond Gate Hyde Pk

NEW ITEM

1 Rutland Gate - Hyde Park
15th July 1851,

Dear Sir

Having always received my
payments from "The Illustrated London
News" through the engraver and never
face to face with any other — induced me
to ask you (when you happened to be
in the City) to obtain it for me.
On occasions of drawing from a picture
the price paid has been £5 or guineas,
and where it has been from a play
or Opera it has been 3 guis. therefore
the amount I imagine to be coming to me
for "the ~~departure~~ representation of the Britons

At the departure of the Romans
would be the former one viz.
guns. the which if you will
kindly receive for me I shall
feel that I am

Your very obliged &c

[signature]

Joseph L. Williams Esq.

NEW ITEM

21 Rutland Gate.
Hyde Park
10th Oct. 1867.

Dear Sir,

The bearer wishes me to
settle a small amount of £5
by cashing his draft on me.
£5.9.0 . will you kindly pay
the amount over by Henry
for Mudie's London. Sons ?
This acknowledgment for me will oblige

Yours very truly
J. Rwantbury Overbeck

William Esq.

—— Williams Esq.
25
Victoria Road.

NEW ITEM

21 Rutland Gate. Hyde Park
31st March 1852.

Madam

Not wishing to cause Mr. Kean the annoyance (should he still be unwell) of reading a note I have taken the liberty of addressing this to you to ask whether Mr. Kean could bear my presence in his room, provided I trouble him not to speak. and if so — when?

I have the honor to be
Madam
Your very obedt.
Servt.
Edward H. Corbould.

Mrs. Charles Kean.

Ingram Content Group UK Ltd.
Milton Keynes UK
UKHW021307300323
419415UK00015B/148